THE CURIOUS SIGN

SCOTT BLACKWELL

SYDNEY · YOUNGSTOWN

The Curious Sign
© Scott Blackwell 2016

All rights reserved. Except as may be permitted by the Copyright Act, no part of this publication may be reproduced in any form or by any means without prior permission from the publisher. Please direct all copyright enquiries and permission requests to the publisher.

Matthias Media
(St Matthias Press Ltd ACN 067 558 365)
Email: info@matthiasmedia.com.au
Internet: www.matthiasmedia.com.au
Please visit our website for current postal and telephone contact information.

Matthias Media (USA)
Email: sales@matthiasmedia.com
Internet: www.matthiasmedia.com
Please visit our website for current postal and telephone contact information.

Scripture quotations are from the Holy Bible, English Standard Version® (ESV®), copyright © 2001 by Crossway, a publishing ministry of Good News Publishers. Used by permission. All rights reserved.

ISBN 978 1 925424 01 0

Cover design and typesetting by Lankshear Design.

CONTENTS

1. Red sky 5
2. The sixpence 11
3. The curious sign 17
4. Lying in a food bin 31
5. The manger 39
6. A sign for you to read 49
7. My Christmas invitation to you... 55

Appendix: The Gospel of Luke
(chapter 2, verses 1-20) 57

① RED SKY

I REMEMBER VERY clearly a curious experience I had as a small boy with my dad. I was standing next to him on the verandah of my uncle's house in Queensland (north east Australia). It was a home surrounded by sugarcane fields as far as the eye could see. The late afternoon sky was aflame with the most astonishing array of colours, but mostly it was crimson red. My dad was smiling, and as he rubbed his big meaty hand on my blonde head he said, "Red sky at night, shepherd's delight".

"Huh?" I said.

He looked down, grinned and said, "Red sky, Scotty. Red sky at night is a shepherd's delight. A red sky in the morning is a shepherd's warning."

"Ah..." I said.

He still grinned. "Signs, Scotty, signs. You gotta know how to read 'em."

At that moment I thought my dad must have been the smartest person in the universe.

After that, the reading and interpreting of signs became a bit of a hobby for me, although I was not nearly as good at it as my older brothers and sister. Compared to them I was a bit of a slow poke in the art form. They could tell, for example, just by the sound of my dad's footsteps coming in from work whether he was in a good mood or a bad one. One minute we would all be sitting in the lounge room making a noisy mess and the next I would be on my own in the midst of toys and games with paper slowly wafting down to the floor. Suddenly there was Dad at the door bellowing like an ogre, "Are you responsible for this pigsty? Clean it up!"

Signs, you gotta know how to read 'em.

I got much better at reading signs as I got older, but with the passing of time I discovered that the whole 'red sky' thing had almost no relevance to Australian weather patterns at all. Apparently it was a sure thing if you were in the northern hemisphere though (say… England). I also discovered that not all signs are subtle, and some are downright rude.

A case in point is a common sign used by the Department of Roads. This government body cannot afford the luxury of subtlety and I suspect that they deliberately employ people who have been blessed with absolutely no sense of social delicacy or restraint in the designing of their road signs. I mean, how much sensitivity do you need in order to place a road sign with its back to the oncoming traffic that reads:

> TURN AROUND. YOU ARE GOING THE WRONG WAY.

Some signs, well, they just shout the obvious. However, of course there is no cure for stupidity and in a world where careless and stupid people exist, *nothing* is obvious. This was driven home to me by a picture of a clothing label that a friend posted on their social media page. It was the label off a baby's jumpsuit. The label read:

WARM HAND WASH.
COOL TUMBLE DRY.
REMOVE CHILD FROM CLOTHING.

This is the result of living in a litigious society. Cafés must be especially careful to put signs on cups of coffee, tea and hot chocolate so that stupid people realize they contain "very hot liquid". Manufacturers must place labels on clothing lest children be idly thrown into washing machines when the garments they are wearing become soiled.

I am, however, sometimes wonderfully heartened by the odd smart alec who will occasionally erect a sign which reads something like:

In case of emergency
RUN LIKE CRAZY!

Or:

Need help? 1. Push red button.
2. Yell "Help" loudly.

Or:

Illiterate? Write to the address below
for assistance.

Other signs are more subtle, like a tone of voice or the sound of tired parental footsteps. They require awareness and they caution you about what dangers may be lurking for the careless. However, the response to the warning is entirely up to you.

These are a bit like the signs near the cliff edge at scenic lookouts:

DANGER. GO NO FURTHER.

You can, of course, distrust the sign and go closer to the edge if you wish, but then there is an increasing possibility that you might die a horrible and grizzly death.

Then there are signs like my dad's 'red sky' that are portents of things to come, and these are always open to broad interpretation... and misinterpretation. The Department of Roads does not waste its time with these.

Signs, you've gotta know how to read 'em. And how not to. And who to trust.

② THE SIXPENCE

Being the youngest in a family of six kids has its advantages and disadvantages. Perhaps the greatest advantage is that you learn to grow up very quickly, and by 'growing up' I mean that you learn how to read people, assess situations and run for cover. I've already confessed that in the beginning I was not particularly skilled in these areas of personal development, but boy oh boy did I learn, and learn fast.

As I think back on my childhood development now, there are scenes and situations that come back to me which still amaze me… and there are some which still make me shake my head in grim astonishment. But the memories that fascinate me most as an adult are my memories of Christmas.

When you are the youngest of six children growing up in a low-income, working-class family, Christmas is rarely about the number and value of gifts that arrive on the day. Instead, it is very much about unexpected surprises and the most astonishing meal prepared by a mother who would create a feast from supplies that you did not even know were in the cupboards.

If you asked, "What is your greatest memory of Christmas as a child?", my answer would be exactly the same as that of my four brothers and my sister. It would be the homemade plum pudding and custard that my mother created each year. Decades later, I can still taste how glorious and wonderful that pudding was; but even more glorious was that in one slice of the pudding, a sixpence had been inserted, and we had no idea who would receive it. A sixpence! As a boy at the age of five in the mid 1960s, a sixpence would buy you more sweets and treats at the local corner store than you could ever imagine. A sixpence... I could be rich!

But that wasn't the highlight of this particular Christmas dessert.

As the custard-bathed pudding arrived, and a dessert bowl was placed in front of each of us, not one of us would touch our spoon and begin to eat. We would wait. We would wait until our father started eating, because at some point, at some stage during dessert, we knew he would begin to cough gently. Then the coughing would get louder, deeper and more desperate. Finally he would croak out, "A sixpence! I've swallowed a flamin' sixpence!" and through roaring family laughter, we would then devour our Christmas pudding, and see which one of us got the actual prize.

That was Christmas Day for my family and me.

Goodness, how Christmas has changed since I was five years old. It seems that these modern Christmas days have virtually nothing to do with creating an opportunity for a family to sit and share a moment of gentle joy together. Today it is more about what I bought you and where I bought it. How much it cost, or how fashionable or socially acceptable it is. And the shopping… good Lord! The horror of Christmas shopping!

For all of these nightmares I blame the character and concept of Santa Claus. Here is a legend about a person who visits your home and delivers you gifts based upon the general positiveness of your behaviour. Originally, this tradition was based on the legend of St Nicholas, a Christian bishop in Turkey who made a life out of helping the poor and needy. As a small boy my positive impression of Santa Claus lasted until I was about three years old, which was roughly the time my older brothers and sister got sick of pretending there was a special secret man visiting the house in December. Now, for me at the age of three, that was a problem. Little did I know that there was a bigger problem I was soon going to have to deal with.

His name was Jesus.

The older I got, the more I began to understand the Bible stories that I was being taught Sunday by Sunday in the church our family went to. Consequently, the older I got, the more I began to grumble when December looked like coming around again. Why? Because I was beginning to learn, in no uncertain terms, that Christmas actually had nothing to do with that overweight old man named Santa. Rather, it had everything to do with the birth of a baby named Jesus.

As a child growing up in a Christian family, Jesus was not a stranger to me. I'd been hearing stories about him forever. But suddenly things were seriously out of order. The conversation with my Sunday School teacher went pretty simply like this:

> "Are you seriously telling me that Christmas is really all about Jesus and his being born somewhere, and has never really had anything to do with Santa Claus? Why? Why? WHY?"

It was from the age of about eight that I seriously left Christmas behind and started to ignore churches as much as I could. I wanted nothing to do with either of them. I knew that there was no Santa, and that the Christmas events my parents had promoted were just a game to keep the family in line and reasonably jolly together. They now owned an eight-year-old boy who had learned how to secretly sneer, how to quietly scowl, and—having somehow discovered the character of Scrooge—how to mutter "Bah humbug!"

For me, Christmas became that time of the year which most of the modern Western society now experiences. It became a time of endurance, because I couldn't really understand it, couldn't really embrace it, and was reluctant to shell out the pocket money I had been saving to join it.

Christmas? Bah humbug!

Oh Scrooge, how I understood you. At least, I thought I did.

③
AN UNEXPECTED SIGN

AT THE AGE OF EIGHTEEN I committed my life to Jesus and became an actual Christian. And, as an actual Christian, I was hopeless. So I did it again at the age of twenty-one and this time I really meant it, and it really stuck.

Now, I know that given the last part you've just read, this is probably a bit of a shock. In truth, it was initially a surprise to me as well. Being a Christian wasn't something I had gone hunting for as I grew from teenager to adult, but it happened, and I have never regretted it.

As a consequence, I have spent a lot of my adult life reading the stories of Jesus and the rest of the Bible.

It's a book that is chock-a-block full of signs and warnings and prophecies, and for me during my early years as a Christian the Bible was like a huge million-piece jigsaw puzzle that I was challenged to solve. Of course, I didn't have anywhere near the tools I needed to find all the solutions, but the basic big message was clear, and I cottoned on to that one pretty quickly.

In the part of the Bible known as the New Testament, the writers make it clear that God has sent his one and only Son to us. He sent him to live a life of obedience that I could never live. More than that, he sent him to die in my place. God sent his son as a sacrifice to secure the forgiveness I needed because of my self-obsession and my rejection of the God who loved and created me. The Son of God was sent to live among us with the task of repairing my broken relationship with God the Father, and to rescue me from the judgement that I genuinely deserved from him. The biography (or Gospel or 'good news') of Jesus written by John in the Bible is crystal clear on this point:

> "For God so loved the world, that he gave his only Son, that whoever believes in

him should not perish but have eternal life. For God did not send his Son into the world to condemn the world, but in order that the world might be saved through him." (John chapter 3, verses 16-17)

That Son who was sent—his name is Jesus. And it was the same Jesus I had known since I was a child.

Interestingly, what this quotation from John's writings in the Bible seems to imply is that the arrival of Jesus himself is a seriously significant sign. It implies that he is *the* great sign of God's plans—his love, his commitment, his compassion.

These truths about the God who rules the universe are all combined and displayed in the life and words of one man: Jesus—the living, breathing, walking, talking sign of God.

The Department of Roads should have suspended one of those big yellow and black, diamond-shaped signs above his head saying: "CAUTION: God At Work!"

What I came to understand as an adult, which I had no capacity to understand when I was a child, was that this whole story begins (in the

New Testament part of the Bible at least) at the time that we celebrate as 'Christmas'.

Now, it was a story that, in theory, I knew well. I could sing the carols and everything! Joseph and Mary, Bethlehem, the shepherds in the fields, the choir of angels, the stable and the baby in the manger, the three wise men—I had all of that down pat. There was only one problem. Well, several actually.

When I read this story[1] again as an adult—as a Christian—I just couldn't make sense of it. It is a story that poses so many questions, but doesn't seem to give many answers. Why shepherds? Why a stable? And what on earth is a 'manger' and why should anybody care? For years and years, I just couldn't figure it out. Let me explain what I mean.

Issue one: Shepherds

In chapter two of the account given by Luke of Jesus' life, there are shepherds in the fields outside Bethlehem on the night Jesus is born. They

---

1   Most of the story I am referring to in this book can be read in Luke's biography of Jesus in the Bible, the Christmas part of which is reproduced in the appendix at the end of this book.

are there to oversee and care for flocks of sheep, protecting them from predatory beasts and other thieves.

This on its own is hard for a 21st-century Australian to get their head around, because sheep farming in Australia is not like this. These days we don't even call the people who look after sheep 'shepherds'. They're sheep farmers... like... pig farmers. In Australia, 'shepherds' have no emotional or personal connection to their sheep as individuals (unless all of them die at once in a drought or a flood—then they might get a bit emotional). Firstly, this is because there can be thousands of sheep in any one flock, and they are not the cuddly kind of sheep that Mary (of nursery rhyme fame) would take to school. They are dirty, paddock and bush roaming creatures. And they smell bad. Secondly, the sheep farmers will round them up using motor bikes and riding horses, then treat them pretty roughly when it comes time for shearing, worming, or drenching. Sheep farming in Australia is not pretty, and if you lose a few of the flock to foxes or dogs... well, they are just sheep. You've got plenty more. You certainly don't sleep out in the paddock at night to protect them.

But in the first century, when Jesus lived, shepherding was a personal thing. The flocks were small, and they were a communal investment and concern. They provided wool for a family's clothing and meat for their food. If there was a scattering of goats among them, then you had access to milk as well. Each shepherd knew every one of the sheep in his care, maybe even by name. He would call or whistle, and they would come running. It was almost like they were domestic pets in some strange, 'out-doorsy' way.

At night, various local shepherds would join their flocks together for safety and convenience, and together, they would watch over each other's animals, taking turns to sleep and eat and so on. In the first century, the shepherd's job was a job of serious communal responsibility, and every sheep was important.

The sheep may have been important, but the shepherds definitely weren't. They lived outside the city, fringe dwellers doing a lowly paid and unglamorous job. They certainly weren't the people you'd expect would receive an announcement of seismic significance. So why do the angels appear to *them*? Why *shepherds*?

But then there was another issue.

Issue two: Prestige

In our modern culture, we love to froth and bubble over things that are impressive. It's how we are as a society and there is no point denying it. We like to know about impressive people. We are obsessed with people whose looks are impressive—the Angelina Jolies, the Cate Blanchetts, the Hugh Jackmans and those innumerable Hemsworth brothers. We just love them, we want to look like them, we want to move like them and dress like them. We want to *be* them.

But we also want to know about people whose intellect is impressive. After all, 'smart' is now the new 'sexy'… it's the new 'cool'. Make room mindless, muscle-bound jock and say "Hello!" shapeless IT nerd, home-brewing and latte-sipping chess whizz. How else can you explain the 'hipster with a little dog' phenomenon?

Most impressive of all, however, is money. We drool over people whose incomes are impressive—the Murdoch dynasty, the Kardashians and Bill Gates. Rich equals impressive, and as long as you are rich you can be famous, even when you have no discernible skills, talents or gifts.

The newspapers, countless magazines, the paparazzi and an entire industry of voyeurism all feed on our infatuation with that which is socially, physically, economically and intellectually impressive. We like to be impressed by people, and we like to impress others. Prestige is important to us. Doing the right things, being seen with the right people, wearing the right clothes, playing the right sport, earning the right money.

And therein lies my second difficulty with the Christmas story. This story presents a situation that is a complete rebuke to all of that material obsessiveness and passion.

The baby we are told about in this story is the one who is proclaimed as both Christ and Lord.

> "Fear not, for behold, I bring you good news of great joy that will be for all the people. For unto you is born this day in

the city of David a Saviour, who is Christ the Lord." (Luke chapter 2, verses 10-11)

The word 'Christ' means king, because this baby is apparently the one who will be the new King over all creation. The word 'Lord' that is coupled with 'Christ' means the one who is in charge of all things. 'Lord' is the same word that is used for God himself. In fact, at the time the title 'Christ' was almost universally understood to be the very Son of God himself.

This announcement is, in essence, the declaration of the arrival of the most important and powerful person on the planet.

And he is born in a stable.

Placed in an animals' feeding trough. A 'manger'.

What a shocking contrast the Christmas story of the birth of Jesus is to the cultural pressure to impress (and let's not imagine prestige wasn't important in the first century)! The one whose arrival we celebrate at Christmas was born in a stable. A *stable*!

I am no midwife, but I am almost certain that if you took a poll of the 'Top 100 Places a Woman

Would Like to Give Birth', 'stable' wouldn't even come close. An answer like this would be "Bad luck and thanks for playing!" on *Family Feud*.

Let me make clear what I am talking about here. This is not one of those nice, cuddly and clean, golden-glow barns that you see on the front of nativity scene Christmas cards. The ones you look at and think, "Hey! That looks better than the last place I stayed on holiday with the kids!"

There is nothing romantic about a first-century Middle-Eastern stable. It is a nasty, unsanitary, unhealthy place for a child to be born. It is most likely an open-air affair, little more than one of those picnic sites you see at the park. You know, they have a couple of benches and a roof to keep the rain off (so long as the rain is coming straight down). Who in their right mind would choose to give birth in such a place? And yet this birth, and this place of birth, is a sign. Remember?

Issue three: Which sign and of what?

While I had issues with the choice of the shepherds and the lack of prestige, these in the end were not my real problem with the nativity story. My *real* problem was that while this group of shepherds are doing their job in the paddocks close to town, a band of heavenly angels appear to these lads, and according to Luke's account in the Bible, after declaring the baby to be Christ and Lord, this is what they say:

> "And this will be a sign for you: you will find a baby wrapped in swaddling cloths and lying in a manger." (Luke chapter 2, verse 12)

Did you see it? Something about the birth of Jesus is a SIGN! That is what the angels say: "And this will be a sign…" But which bit, and what kind of sign is it?

I remember reading this for the first time and thinking hard. What part of this is the *actual sign*? It could not possibly be the fact that a baby was born in Bethlehem that night. For heaven's sake, it was census time! There were thousands of people flowing into Bethlehem from all over the nation, and I'm willing to bet that at least a hundred of them would have been heavily pregnant women. The fact that there was a baby born in Bethlehem that night could not possibly have been the sign.

Neither was the fact that the baby was "wrapped in swaddling cloths" likely to be the sign. I mean, everybody wrapped their babies in swaddling clothes during those times in that part of the world. Swaddling cloths were the cotton jumpsuits of the first century. In fact, if you took the swaddling cloths off the baby and looked at the label, you would probably find that it said:

WARM HAND WASH WITH A ROCK
IN THE STREAM.
HANG UPWIND FROM GOATS TO DRY.
REMOVE CHILD FROM CLOTHING.

The sign, therefore, must lie within the final part of this announcement. The actual sign must be the *manger*: "...you will find a baby wrapped in swaddling cloths and *lying in a manger*". Yes, there is a baby born in Bethlehem this night and, yes, he is wrapped in swaddling cloths and is not stark naked. But the truly significant thing is that he is lying in his bed, which is an animals' feeding trough. He is lying in a manger. You only find those in stables.

Now what on earth is a baby in an animals' food trough a sign of... besides the presence of alarmingly poor parenting skills?

④
LYING IN A FOOD BIN

My family happened to live in a suburb of Ipswich in Queensland called Goodna at the time when I was born.

There also happened to be a rather large psychiatric institution in Goodna. It was known as 'The Goodna Asylum'. As you can imagine, facilities for mental health care in 1961 were nothing like they are now, and yes, there was a massive stigma attached to that place.

My older siblings made sure that I understood the stigma perfectly as I grew up. Whenever we would fight or argue, the clinching comment that was always marshalled to ensure my defeat was "Well at least I wasn't born at the Goodna funny farm!" I know, it is shockingly harsh and cruel, but it was the sixties (and my siblings) that we are talking about. This would then be accompanied by the retreating chant of "Scott was born in Goodna! Scott was born in Goodna!"

I didn't ask to be born there, I just was. And I wasn't even born in the asylum anyway! My birth certificate clearly states: "PLACE OF BIRTH: ROYAL BRISBANE HOSPITAL". But it was no use. I was branded. Labelled. Doomed never to be victorious in family conflicts, all because of the place we lived when I was born. It was so accursedly unfair. Even today I still feel a slight twitch in the corner of my left eye when I meet someone who confesses that they are from or have spent time in Goodna.

They say that Winston Churchill was born in a cloakroom (which is a polite name for a cupboard). Mind you, it was a cupboard at Blenheim Palace that just happens to be larger and more luxurious than most people's living rooms. But a cupboard nonetheless. Without these finer details it could seem like a pretty humble beginning for a man who would become one of Britain's most famous and successful leaders—but the details kind of ruin its chances of becoming a really cracking piece of mythology, don't they?

In these modern, politically correct times we don't like to believe that where a person is born will have any impact on the possibility of them fulfilling their greatest potential. In fact, we become quite rowdy in our declarations that all people should be treated equally and be afforded equal opportunity in life. It is a lovely and noble ideal, but it is of course nonsense: the reality falls a long way short. The child born in the slums of Delhi has infinitely more difficulties to face, and as a result far less chance of rising above their circumstances, than someone born anywhere in Blenheim Palace, even if it was a cupboard.

This is why we are so fond of 'the battler'. The whole world loves a story about someone from a down-and-out context who rises above their circumstances and makes a startling success of their lives. We love the self-made men and women of business. We read their books and give them their own television shows. We love those who travel the road of adversity with a grim-faced determination to succeed. We love athletes who overcome terrible injuries or unexpected handicaps in order to write their names in large, proud letters on the world stage. We love kids who live in squalor but who can sing like an angel, who get discovered and go on to become royalty in the entertainment world. We hear these stories and it is like a small piece of hope falls from the sky to warm our hearts.

In this world, it is more often than not true that where you are born *matters*. What country, what city, even what suburb matters. Being born in the wrong place can haunt you and hinder you every day of your life. After all, who would intentionally choose to be born in a slum? Who would choose to carry a lifelong disability? Who would intentionally choose a childhood of hardship and neglect? Who would choose poverty over wealth, or suffering over luxury?

All of these issues bring us back to the problem of the unexpected arrival of the angel-announced Saviour, Christ and Lord, born in Bethlehem. Who would choose to have their child born in a stable and placed in an animals' feeding trough when there was even the remotest possibility of cupboard space anywhere else?

It seems that the God of the Bible would, that's who. But why?

As a new and confused Christian, I began to do some research. But I didn't like what I read because it didn't make any sense—at least not to me anyway. The sign that the angels announced to the shepherds was, I assumed, a sign that shepherds would be able to understand. They were simple people, doing a laborious job. They were not scholars or theologians... or even obstetricians. They were outdoor-living, rough-headed shepherds. It was for this simple reason that I dismissed a fair few of the explanations I initially read from highfalutin religious types.

For example, I read one long proposal arguing that Jesus was placed in an animals' feeding trough as a baby because he would later be understood by the church as 'the bread of heaven' in the services that many churches celebrate called 'the Lord's Supper' (or Holy Communion). Therefore, it was perfectly appropriate for Jesus to be placed in a feeding trough as a baby because the church would later feed on him as a 'holy sacrament'.

Now, I love a nice touch of symbolism as much as the next person... but please, PLEASE! Let's not get carried away with ourselves! I am completely certain that Jesus being placed in the feeding trough has absolutely nothing to do with him actually being considered to be food (symbolic or otherwise). Further, this is hardly the first thing that would have popped into the shepherds' minds when they found the right stable and saw the baby there in the feeding trough. "Oh look lads, supper is on!" No.

I have no doubt that when the shepherds were told that the "Christ" and "Lord" was going to be born and placed in a feeding trough (a manger), they would have been absolutely astonished, and certainly no less amazed when they found him exactly as described. No small part of their amazement would have been because this was a highly unusual place to find someone who had been declared by angels from heaven as "a newborn king".

So let's tone down the symbolism and dial up the reality for a few minutes.

It is one thing to be born into a set of circumstances; it is another thing entirely to be *appointed* to those circumstances. That God appoints these circumstances for the arrival of his Son on earth says something important. It says something about the character of God himself.

What it says, however... well, that is where our need for interpretation comes into play.

It would be easy for us to conclude that this God is at best an irresponsible and at worst a nasty parent for choosing such a place to bring his Son into the world. However my experience and understanding of the God of the Bible is that he is neither nasty nor irresponsible. Could it be that by appointing this place and these circumstances for the birth of his Son, this God is making a specific point and at the same time revealing something profound about his character and his intentions?

But what is that point, and what might we learn about him through this curious sign? What sort of God could he be?

⑤
THE MANGER

THE FIRST THING I want to say is that this child is not *just* a child. The first chapter of John's biography of Jesus makes it clear that this child is *God the Son*—that is, this child is God himself.

> In the beginning was the Word, and the Word was with God, and the Word was God. He was in the beginning with God. All things were made through him, and without him was not any thing made that was made... And the Word became flesh and dwelt among us, and we have seen his glory, glory as of the only Son from the Father, full of grace and truth. (John chapter 1, verses 1-3 and verse 14)

This child is born as the fulfilment of some fairly hefty promises made by God to generations centuries before he arrived. For example, this promise made centuries before:

> For to us a child is born,
>   to us a son is given;
> and the government shall be upon his
>   shoulder,
>   and his name shall be called
> Wonderful Counsellor, Mighty God,
>   Everlasting Father, Prince of Peace.
>   (Isaiah chapter 9, verse 6)

So this baby—whom the angels tell the shepherds is "Christ the Lord"—is also revealed to be God's Son, God in the flesh. Which kind of explains why the wise men walk into a dirty stable, take a look at a pretty standard looking baby lying in an animal food trough, and instead of feeling sorry for him for the humble start he has in life, recognize they need to fall down in his presence and worship him:

> And going into the house they saw the child with Mary his mother, and they

> fell down and worshiped him. Then, opening their treasures, they offered him gifts, gold and frankincense and myrrh.
> (Matthew chapter 2, verse 11)

The child who is born is, in truth, a sign himself.

A sign of the God who has been born

It is a sign that reveals the sort of God who appoints and oversees these events. This is the God who provides a rescuer for all humanity. He himself is that rescuer. It is God himself who comes to us, born in a stable and placed within a manger at that first Christmas. He is the God who becomes a human.

The child born is a sign of the kind of God we should worship.

Now at this point, it is worth pausing. These things are easily said, but they are mind-boggling in their implications. This is like suggesting that a girl from Tasmania can meet a guy in a bar one night in Sydney and as a result, become the princess of Denmark.

It's inconceivable, and yet that is the story

(moderately abbreviated though it might be) of Crown Princess Mary of Denmark. An Aussie girl from the Apple Isle becomes the soon-to-be-queen of a European nation. You can't write fiction that good! And yet as inconceivable as that story might be (I know I keep using that word, and I do know what it means), it does not even begin to touch on the astonishing truths that lie within the Bible, which speaks about the birth of a tiny human child as the arrival to earth of the eternal God of the universe.

Suddenly we are no longer speaking of a distant and impersonal 'Creator God' who watches us but is removed and uninvolved in our conditions or circumstances. In this birth, he is called "Immanuel", which means *"God with us"*, according to the ancient prophet Isaiah and the evangelist Matthew, who wrote the account of Jesus' entire life in his Gospel. This is the God who willingly and purposefully lays aside the garments of his majesty, his might, eternity and glory in order to become something as lowly and accessible as a human. He is the sort of God who doesn't disdain or despise humanity or the human form. Rather, he embraces it. He is the sort of God who does not arrive demanding the palaces and attendants that are his right. No, he is the kind of God who, when he chooses to come among those he has created, also chooses to be born in circumstances that feature humility and accessibility.

Why? Because this God has committed himself to our salvation, and in order to save us he becomes like us. He had made a promise long ago to seek out and save those who were lost and dying as a result of their sin and rebellion. He had given expression to his deep desire to be the good shepherd and faithful overseer of our souls. And so in love and service, the God of the universe takes on human flesh and becomes a man.

Astonishing! Inconceivable! Yet true.

A sign of rejection

But why a stable? Why a manger?

It is important to note that the Christmas story speaks not only of this child's circumstances being humble, but also of these circumstances being brought about for a reason. This birth is not just a scene of humility; it is also a scene of gob-smacking rejection. This baby is born in the stable outside because there was no room at the inn. *Nobody* would give their room to this pregnant mother. Really?

Now Australian society has a bit of a reputation for being a tough kind of place, but I have seen the most hardened, grizzled chauvinist stand up and give his seat to a pregnant woman on public transport. I have seen people with significant disabilities struggle up out of their seats to accommodate an expectant mother. I have seen bumper-to-bumper traffic stop on a main road of Sydney in order to allow a pregnant mum to safely cross. You see, in the end there are just some things that we will not, and cannot be, hard-hearted about. The needs of a pregnant mother appear to be one of them.

But that wasn't the case in Bethlehem that night. Nobody would hand over their room and warm bed to her and her potential child. "You can have the stable, lady." That's one hard, hard town all right.

The Christ-child begins his life in rejection and hardship. If the manger reminds us of anything, it reminds us that the God of glory chose to come to earth, and in coming he chose to lay his glory aside. God chose humility and the circumstances of poverty, hardship and rejection for his arrival.

But what do we learn? In these circumstances we learn that despite all the hate-filled atheistic railing against God, and despite all the accusations of ignorance and enslavement, the consistent truth about the God of the Bible is that *the greatest mark of this God's glory is his unrelenting and steadfast love*.

What does the curious sign of the manger mean? It means that God loves you so much that he will step away from majesty and choose humility for your sake.

A sign of the work he comes to do

The baby born in a stable is a Saviour. He has come to perform a rescue. This is the first description we are given of him as the angels speak to the shepherds in Luke's story about his birth. Yet

Jesus does not save us simply by being born. This particular part of God's salvation plan is just the beginning. Yet to come are the thirty-three years of his life and ministry. The child grows into a boy, and the boy into a man. He lives, and he preaches and teaches the Good News that now is the time to turn away from our rebellion against God and take the step into his kingdom as beloved sons and daughters.

In essence: "TURN AROUND. YOU ARE GOING THE WRONG WAY."

The Bible tells us that people are drawn from every part of the nation in which Jesus lived, and they commit themselves to him as their Lord and Saviour. They believe that he is, in truth, the promised Christ and Lord.

But as he preaches and teaches about the kingdom of his Father in heaven, others are stirred up to anger and violence against him. You see, he challenges their comfort. He challenges their authority. He challenges the things they teach about God and the way that they present themselves as being on the inside track to God's blessing. Eventually, it is these people who will make false accusations about him, slander his reputation, seize him, arrest him, judge him and murder him by nailing him to a wooden cross.

And just as he was born as a Saviour in rejection, so he will die rejected.

Here is yet another dimension to the curious sign that is the manger. In a very real sense this birth in a barn and his placement within an animals' feeding trough is a foretelling, a foreshadowing if you will, of the greater rejection that this child will suffer in his adult death. It is a rejection that he was destined to suffer. It is difficult for many people to understand this part of the plan and purpose of God, but the reason for Jesus' birth is not simply the stable image of Christmas. Rather it is his endurance of the cross on Good Friday and his absence from the empty tomb on Easter Sunday.

This child is born for one reason, and for one reason only: to die in your place for the forgiveness of your sins.

But if this is the case, you must ask yourself: "What took him to that humiliating death and what kept him so resolutely determined to walk toward that cross and that terrible death?"

The answer that the Bible gives is this: it was the same love that brought him to our world in the first place. So much did he love you, he was willing to endure this pain and rejection in order to save you and achieve the possibility of your acceptance, forgiveness and love by God the Father.

> "For even the Son of Man came not to be served but to serve, and to give his life as a ransom for many." (Mark chapter 10, verse 45)

⑥
A SIGN FOR YOU TO READ

Way, way back, when you first started reading this, you might remember that I kept making a particular comment. It was this: *Signs, you gotta know how to read 'em.*

You have to ask, don't you, "Why on earth would you start a Christian story with that, and what could it possibly have to do with me?" The simple answer is this: Christmas is not the fairy story of a red-costumed fat man in a flying sleigh. It is the story of God sending to earth a little baby boy to be born in a barn and discovered whilst sleeping in a manger by shepherds.

Having seen the angels from heaven, and having heard from the God that rules both heaven and earth through them, the shepherds are required to come to terms with this truth:

> "...I bring you good news of a great joy that will be for all the people. For unto you is born this day in the city of David a Saviour, who is Christ the Lord. And this will be a sign for you: you will find a baby wrapped in swaddling cloths and lying in a manger." (Luke chapter 2, verses 10-12)

If the curious sign of the manger speaks of anything, it is that this Jesus—this Lord and Saviour—is humble and lowly of heart. As majestic as he will eventually be revealed to be, the reality is that he will never be too important for you to get to meet, know or understand. You will never be too small or too inferior for him. He is seriously concerned about you.

Yes, he is 'God the Son'. But this is the God who, out of love and compassion, bends down so that he might lift you up and show you how important you truly are in his eyes and within his heart. This is the man who lives a life exactly like yours, but in service to God, and who then surrenders that same life in service to *you*.

Who can fathom a God that would love in such a way? And yet here he is, a baby in a manger who is there so that the people he has come to save might have full and unhindered access to God. He is there in that humble place so that the shepherds can come and see, without hindrance and without fear. He is there for *them*, as simple and ordinary as they are. But, of course, Jesus is not *only* there for the shepherds.

The part of this story recorded in Matthew's account of Jesus' birth in the Bible also speaks of a more prestigious group of people who are also desperately seeking him.

> Now after Jesus was born in Bethlehem of Judea in the days of Herod the king, behold, wise men from the east came to Jerusalem, saying, "Where is he who has been born king of the Jews? For we saw his star when it rose and have come to worship him." (Matthew chapter 2 verses 1-2)

He is God the Son—whom all of us need to honour as our Lord (our king), just as the wise men from the East did. But he was also born to be a blessing to all who meet him and honour him: the rich and the poor, the young and the old, the local and the foreigner. This boy is born so that an amazing blessing from God might come to every man, woman and child who meets him and comes to know him.

What then is the blessing?

Actually, we have already mentioned it. It is the blessing of *forgiveness*, the blessing of *new relationship*, the blessing of *life*.

This is Christmas as it was actually meant to be. And these are the blessings—the precious gifts that were meant to be remembered, celebrated and received with joy.

Christmas is a sign.

The gift is a boy, who will become the man who pays your debt and brings you forgiveness, life and relationship with God, who is both your Creator and your Father.

It is the gift that has been offered to you, not merely one day each year but 365 days a year. And it is the gift that you can receive and accept every day. Any day. Even today.

What then does the phrase 'Merry Christmas' mean? It means you have been brought "good news of great joy". One day in each year, we set time aside so that we might specifically remember the arrival of God's love, forgiveness and blessing—in the form of a little baby boy, lying in a manger.

Christmas is a sign.

Signs, you gotta know how to read 'em.

MY CHRISTMAS INVITATION TO YOU...

Friends, I want to invite you to take this opportunity to live out this Christmas, and every day for the rest of your life, in a new and personal relationship with Jesus. I want to invite you to receive the gift God offers you:

> But to all who did receive him, who believed in his name, he gave the right to become children of God... (John chapter 1, verse 12)

I invite you to accept this gift.

All you need to do is ask God, and the gift that you didn't think you needed—Jesus as Lord of your life and God as your heavenly Father—can be yours.

Here is a personal prayer that you might find helpful...

Heavenly Father,

I know that I have let my life drift away from you. I have left you out of my life, ignored you, and tried to go it alone, and for this I am truly sorry. Please forgive me.

Lord, I want to come back into a right relationship with you and start again.

I want to accept the gift of life and of welcome into your family.

From today on, I want to live as your person.

Amen.

God bless and merry Christmas!

APPENDIX

The Gospel of Luke, chapter 2, verses 1-20
The Birth of Jesus Christ

[1] In those days a decree went out from Caesar Augustus that all the world should be registered. [2] This was the first registration when Quirinius was governor of Syria. [3] And all went to be registered, each to his own town. [4] And Joseph also went up from Galilee, from the town of Nazareth, to Judea, to the city of David, which is called Bethlehem, because he was of the house and lineage of David, [5] to be registered with Mary, his betrothed, who was with child. [6] And while they were there, the time came for her to give birth. [7] And she gave birth to her firstborn son and wrapped him in swaddling cloths and

laid him in a manger, because there was no place for them in the inn.

The Shepherds and the Angels

[8] And in the same region there were shepherds out in the field, keeping watch over their flock by night. [9] And an angel of the Lord appeared to them, and the glory of the Lord shone around them, and they were filled with great fear. [10] And the angel said to them, "Fear not, for behold, I bring you good news of great joy that will be for all the people. [11] For unto you is born this day in the city of David a Saviour, who is Christ the Lord. [12] And this will be a sign for you: you will find a baby wrapped in swaddling cloths and lying in a manger." [13] And suddenly there was with the angel a multitude of the heavenly host praising God and saying,

> [14] "Glory to God in the highest,
> and on earth peace among those with
> whom he is pleased!"

[15] When the angels went away from them into heaven, the shepherds said to one another, "Let

us go over to Bethlehem and see this thing that has happened, which the Lord has made known to us." [16] And they went with haste and found Mary and Joseph, and the baby lying in a manger. [17] And when they saw it, they made known the saying that had been told them concerning this child. [18] And all who heard it wondered at what the shepherds told them. [19] But Mary treasured up all these things, pondering them in her heart. [20] And the shepherds returned, glorifying and praising God for all they had heard and seen, as it had been told them.

Also from Matthias Media

Can we trust what the Gospels say about Jesus?

Jesus is an amazing man; he changed human history. But can you really know anything about him? Hasn't the Bible been changed over the centuries? Aren't Christians just making it all up? In his careful, balanced, but immensely readable way, Andrew Errington looks at some of the big questions surrounding the history of Jesus. This is a booklet full of evidence, challenges and surprising conclusions. For example, did you know that the authors of the Bible were biased, and that's precisely why you should read them?

Short enough to read but long enough to tackle the big questions, this booklet deals with the origins of the gospel stories about Jesus; how they got to us today; and evidence for Jesus from outside the Bible. If you've ever wondered what the Bible actually is, or why it's worth reading, then this is for you.

For more information or to order contact:

Matthias Media
Email: sales@matthiasmedia.com.au
www.matthiasmedia.com.au

Matthias Media (USA)
Email: sales@matthiasmedia.com
www.matthiasmedia.com

Also from Matthias Media

The Essential Jesus

The Gospel of Jesus is for all sorts of readers.

You may be wondering what life is all about, and whether there are any answers to the questions you have.

You may be quite sceptical about Christianity and religion in general, but curious to know what Jesus himself taught.

You may know that there is a God, but not know how to have a relationship with him.

You may have grown up with some sort of Christian background, but not have read the story of Jesus for yourself.

Whoever you are, and whatever your beliefs and background, reading the Gospel of Jesus (as Luke tells it) is an opportunity to get back to the real Jesus, *the essential Jesus*, and to discover something new about yourself, about your world and about God.

FOR MORE INFORMATION OR TO ORDER CONTACT:

Matthias Media
Email: sales@matthiasmedia.com.au
www.matthiasmedia.com.au

Matthias Media (USA)
Email: sales@matthiasmedia.com
www.matthiasmedia.com

Also from Matthias Media

The Book of Books

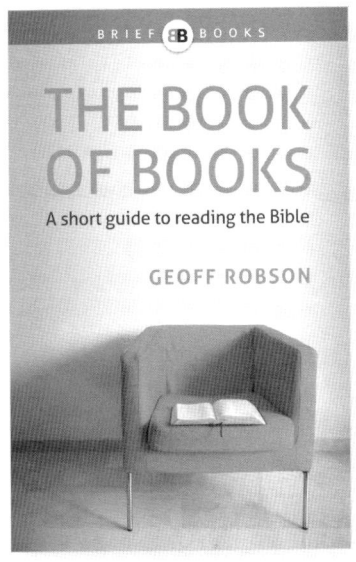

At one level, the Bible is such an outstanding publishing success story that, just by the sheer scale of its translation and the quantities printed, it calls out to every person on the planet: *"Read me!"*

Add to that the profound impact the Bible has had on our culture, and the personal testimony of the many who claim it has transformed their lives, and the case to open and read it surely becomes compelling.

But… the barriers to doing so can be off-putting.

It's a big book, written a long time ago, with words and ideas that may be unfamiliar to us. Where do I start? How do I go about it? Can I trust that what I am reading is the original, uncompromised Bible? How do all the different sections fit together and relate to each other?

Geoff Robson writes to help you read the Bible, answering these and other common questions and explaining how to go about it and get the most out of it.

FOR MORE INFORMATION OR TO ORDER CONTACT:

Matthias Media
Email: sales@matthiasmedia.com.au
www.matthiasmedia.com.au

Matthias Media (USA)
Email: sales@matthiasmedia.com
www.matthiasmedia.com

Matthias Media is an independent Christian publishing company based in Sydney, Australia. To browse our online catalogue, access samples and free downloads, and find more information about our resources, visit our website:

www.matthiasmedia.com

How to buy our resources

1. Direct from us over the internet:
   - in the US: www.matthiasmedia.com
   - in Australia: www.matthiasmedia.com.au

2. Direct from us by phone: please visit our website for current phone contact information.

3. Through a range of outlets in various parts of the world. Visit **www.matthiasmedia.com/contact** for details about recommended retailers in your part of the world.

4. Trade enquiries can be addressed to:
   - in the US and Canada: sales@matthiasmedia.com
   - in Australia and the rest of the world: sales@matthiasmedia.com.au